The Grapes of Wrath

Lightbox Literature Studies

John Perritano and Katie Gillespie

LIGHTBOX
openlightbox.com

LIGHTBOX

Go to
www.openlightbox.com
and enter this book's
unique code.

ACCESS CODE

LBXK6267

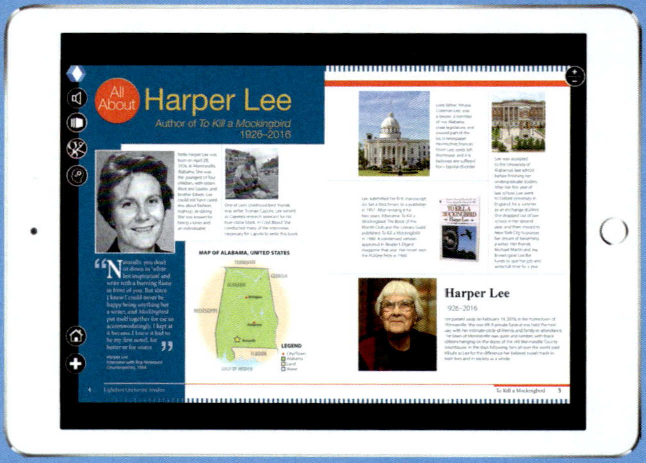

Lightbox is an all-inclusive digital solution for the teaching and learning of curriculum topics in an original, groundbreaking way. Lightbox is based on National Curriculum Standards.

STANDARD FEATURES OF LIGHTBOX

AUDIO High-quality narration using text-to-speech system

VIDEOS Embedded high-definition video clips

ACTIVITIES Printable PDFs that can be emailed and graded

WEBLINKS Curated links to external, child-safe resources

SLIDESHOWS Pictorial overviews of key concepts

TRANSPARENCIES Step-by-step layering of maps, diagrams, charts, and timelines

INTERACTIVE MAPS Interactive maps and aerial satellite imagery

QUIZZES Ten multiple choice questions that are automatically graded and emailed for teacher assessment

KEY WORDS Matching key concepts to their definitions

MORE Extra information and details on the subject

FIRST HAND Letters, diaries, and other primary sources

DOCS Speeches, newspaper articles, and other historical documents

Contents

2 Access Lightbox Student Edition
4 All About John Steinbeck
6 Setting of the Novel
8 Time Period of the Novel
10 Conflict in the Novel
12 Introducing the Characters
14 The Art of Storytelling
16 Theme in the Novel
18 Symbolism in the Novel
20 The Use of Language
22 Impact of the Novel at the Time of Publishing
24 Impact of the Novel Now
26 Perspectives on Economic Uncertainty in the United States
28 Writing a Comparative Essay
30 Key Words/Literary Terms
31 Index
32 Log on to www.openlightbox.com

RUBRIC

Conducting an Interview

Students will conduct an interview with a community member about a time period in their community's history, and submit an audio recording and transcript of the interview. An exemplary interview will meet the following criteria.

- Clearly defines the purpose of the interview
- Conducts thorough background research to inform the focus of the interview and the questions
- Drafts a complete list of thoughtful, in-depth, and varied questions prior to the interview
- Interviews a subject with relevant knowledge on the topic and time period in question
- Asks questions in a logical order, building upon each other
- Treats the interview subject in a polite, respectful, and professional manner
- Does not interrupt or rush the interview subject
- Shows interest and enthusiasm in responses and follow-up questions
- Chooses follow-up questions that demonstrate active listening
- Asks for clarification and further details when necessary
- Asks questions about personal experiences related to the topic
- Asks questions regarding factual information and the interview subject's opinion on the topic
- Asks creative questions that reflect fresh insights on the topic
- Records the full interview in a quiet environment
- Organizes and edits the interview transcript to be clear and factual

All About

John Steinbeck

Author of *The Grapes of Wrath*
1902–1968

John Steinbeck was born on February 27, 1902, in Salinas, California, in a fertile valley that would provide the backdrop for some of his best-known novels. Growing up, Steinbeck was seemingly content, and his family, which included his parents and three sisters, lived modestly. His father, John Ernst Steinbeck, owned a feed-and-grain store and a flour mill, and also **dabbled** in politics, serving as treasurer of Monterey County. Steinbeck's mother, Olive, was a former school teacher. When he was 14, Steinbeck often locked himself in his bedroom to write stories and poems.

"Critics dare you to be 'great.' But this is all after the fact. You didn't want to be great. You just wanted to write a book and have people read it. I have had some very strange criticism. Let's take the inner chapters of *The Grapes of Wrath*. They have been **pommeled**...The reader in general accepted them for what they were. A writer who spends that much time on a book usually knows what he is doing and why. Critics refuse to believe this."

Letter from John Steinbeck to Columbia University student Herbert Sturz, 1953

MAP OF THE UNITED STATES

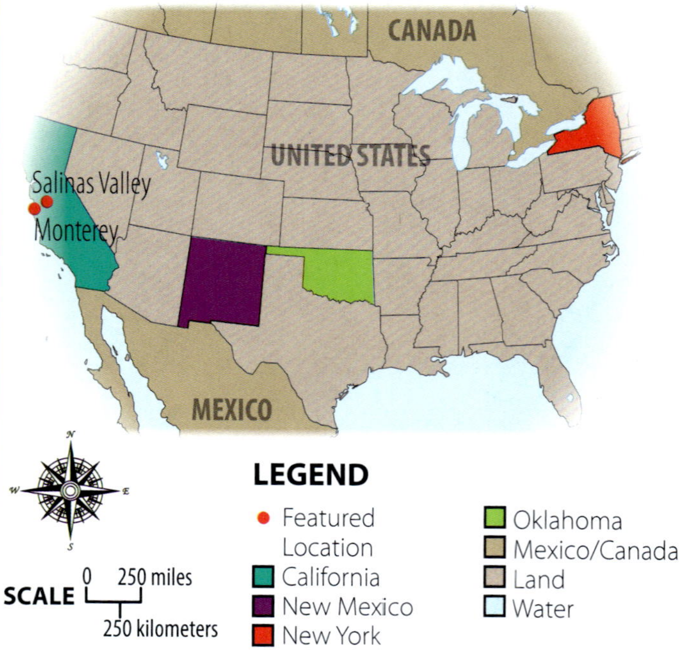

Steinbeck was a smart, shy child who loved the land, particularly the **verdant** fields of Salinas Valley. He dropped in and out of college, finally leaving in 1925 without a degree. Once he was out of school, Steinbeck moved to New York City to pursue a career in writing. Money was tight, so he took jobs as a newspaper reporter and a construction worker, writing stories in his spare time. After being unable to find a publisher for his stories, Steinbeck moved back to California.

Steinbeck published his first novel, *Cup of Gold*, in 1929, and married his first wife, Carol Henning, the following year. She worked hard and brought home a paycheck while her husband wrote feverishly. Steinbeck's early work did not attract much attention, and it was not until *Tortilla Flat,* an often funny story about the adventures of a group of Mexican-American men in Monterey, California, that Steinbeck found critical acclaim. He then wrote other popular books, including the novella *Of Mice and Men*, which was published in 1937.

In 1939, Steinbeck achieved his greatest success with *The Grapes of Wrath*, an instant classic that told the story of a **dispossessed** family from Oklahoma and their struggle to find a new life in California at the height of the Great Depression. The book was a critical success, as it captured the mood of Americans who were struggling under the same conditions. For a time, the book sold an astounding 10,000 copies a week, and earned Steinbeck a Pulitzer Prize in 1940. He followed that success with other memorable novels, including *Cannery Row* in 1945, *East of Eden* in 1952, and *The Winter of Our Discontent* in 1961.

Steinbeck died of heart disease on December 20, 1968, at his home in New York City. His simple funeral at St. James's Episcopal Church was attended by many from the circles of show business and literature. Among those in attendance was actor Henry Fonda, who starred as Tom Joad in the film version of *The Grapes of Wrath*. Fonda read several of Steinbeck's favorite poems at the funeral, including *Ulysses* by Alfred Lord Tennyson.

ACTIVITIES

Google Maps

Route 66, United States

Explore the Mother Road that the Joad family took from Oklahoma to California, using street view.

First Hand

Interview with John Steinbeck

Examine this 1952 audio interview with John Steinbeck.

1. What types of questions does the interviewer ask? What topics does he focus on? Why would he focus on these specific areas?
2. The interviewer says that it would be understandable if the people who left the Dust Bowl felt hate and loathing for the land. How does Steinbeck respond to this suggestion? Do you agree with his assessment of the situation? Why or why not?

RUBRIC

Researching for a Writing Assignment

Students will complete a thorough research process to prepare for a writing assignment, and organize their research in a logical manner that supports their writing. An exemplary research process will meet the following criteria.

- Creates a goal for the research, based on the topic and working thesis
- Creates specific, thoughtful, and inventive research questions that are relevant to the topic of the writing assignment
- Produces a list of categories, key words, and related ideas to effectively assist in researching
- Uses high-quality sources that pertain to the topic and come in a variety of formats, such as books, journals, primary sources, websites, and databases
- Determines accuracy of all sources
- Uses sources that provide balanced research and various perspectives on the topic in question
- Takes notes to highlight the key facts and ideas in order to answer all research questions
- Extracts relevant, detailed information from the sources during the note-taking process
- Organizes the research notes in a clear and concise manner
- Organizes the research notes logically and in a way that sets up the information and ideas for analysis and the writing process
- Analyzes the information and produces ideas and points to support the working thesis
- Uses an effective and suitable format to present all research
- Properly cites all sources used

Setting of the Novel

The Grapes of Wrath is set mostly in the Dust Bowl state of Oklahoma, on Route 66, and in the fields of California. At the time Steinbeck wrote the novel, a severe drought had Oklahoma and the rest of the Great Plains in its deadly grip. The area had been over-farmed after World War I, and by the 1930s, the land was dry and cracked as crops withered and died. The loose topsoil, no longer anchored by plant roots, blew away, and huge dust storms engulfed the region. Entire farms were left barren, forcing many people to pack their belongings and leave the area.

Snapshot

During the Great Depression, Oklahoma lost **440,000 residents to migration**.

1.5 million Oklahomans lived in **rural areas** in the 1930s.

Winds on Black Sunday reached speeds **up to 60 miles per hour. (97 kilometers per hour)**

The Dust Bowl

"To the red country and part of the gray country of Oklahoma, the last rains came gently, and they did not cut the scarred earth…The last rains lifted the corn quickly and scattered weed colonies and grass along the sides of the roads so that the gray country and the dark red country began to disappear under a green cover. In the last part of May the sky grew pale and the clouds that had hung in high puffs for so long in the spring were dissipated. The sun flared down on the growing corn day after day until a line of brown spread along the edge of each green bayonet. The clouds appeared, and went away, and in a while they did not try any more."

Chapter 1

The term "Dust Bowl" was coined in 1935, in the wake of the one of the largest dust storms to hit the region—Black Sunday. It was on April 14, 1935, that a tremendous dust storm blackened the sky, turning a pleasant and sunny Sunday afternoon into a dark night. Fueled by fast winds, the storm blackened the sky in the Great Plains region.

Robert E. Greiger, a reporter for the Associated Press, penned an article the day after Black Sunday that appeared in the *Lubbock Evening Journal*. "Residents of the southwestern dust bowl marked up another black duster today," he wrote. Another Associated Press story described the event by noting that, "Three little words...rule life in the dust bowl of the continent—'if it rains.'"

ACTIVITIES

Document

Steinbeck's People in Flight: an Analysis of the Transformative Forces of the Road Taken
Analyze the January 2015 article by Petra Purkrábková.

1. In the article, Purkrábková says that the first chapter of *The Grapes of Wrath* "sets the somber and melancholic mood." In what ways does Steinbeck establish this mood? How does the mood change over the course of the novel? Why do you think this is the case? Cite passages from the novel to support your answer.
2. Why do you think Steinbeck chose to open the novel in Oklahoma? How does this affect the reader's understanding of the Joads' situation and that of the other "Okies"?

Weblink

On the 'Grapes of Wrath' Trail, the Dust Bowl Still Resonates
Review the *National Geographic* article by Barbara Paulsen, published on December 29, 2014.

1. In the article, Paulsen explains that when writing *The Grapes of Wrath*, Steinbeck consulted a map that he had used himself on a trip along Route 66, years before. In what ways might his personal experiences have influenced the way he describes the setting in the novel? How reliable are such memories when it comes to recounting specific details?
2. One of Paulsen's goals was to "investigate whether history might be repeating itself." Do you think this is the case? Why? Explain your answer.

Time Period of the Novel

The Grapes of Wrath was written during the Great Depression, a time of economic upheaval that began in 1929 with the stock market crash on October 29, and lasted until the end of the 1930s. The crash destroyed the livelihoods of millions, including the very wealthy and the very poor. People lost their homes, farms, and businesses, savings accounts were wiped out, and banks were closed.

Hard Times

"'People gonna have a look in their eye. They gonna look at you an' their face says, 'I don't like you...' You gonna see in people's face how they hate you. An'—I'll tell you somepin. They hate you 'cause they're scairt. They know a hungry fella gonna get food even if he got to take it. They know that fallow lan's a sin an' somebody' gonna take it...'
Tom looked down into the water, and he dug his heels into the sand.
'S'pose a fella got work an' saved, couldn' he get a little lan'?'
The older man laughed and he looked at his boy, and his silent boy grinned almost in triumph. And the man said, 'You ain't gonna get no steady work. Gonna scrabble for your dinner ever' day. An' you gonna do her with people lookin' mean at you.'"

Chapter 18

The Great Depression began when Herbert Hoover was president of the United States. As it worsened, Hoover refused to allow the government to set up programs that might help the poor and the unemployed. Since many people did not have jobs, they took to the road to find work, and hopefully, a better life. Many went to California, aiming to work on farms and ranches, but these new migrant workers faced stiff competition from those already living in the state. At the time, jobs were scarce, and the migrants faced prejudice and hostility. Those who did not find jobs or places to live formed mini-communities of tents and other shelters in so-called "Hoovervilles." They named these shanty towns after President Hoover, since they blamed him for the Depression.

In 1932, American voters elected a new president, Franklin D. Roosevelt, who took immediate steps to help people. By the time he took office in 1933, 13 million Americans were out of work, most of the banks had failed, and industrial production had dropped. Economic devastation affected not only the United States, but also many other countries such as Canada, France, Great Britain, and Germany.

In the United States, Roosevelt called his economic stimulus program the "New Deal." The government created a number of agencies to provide relief, including the Civilian Conservation Corp (CCC), which put people to work on conservation projects in public parks, and the Works Progress Administration (WPA), through which workers found employment building bridges, roads, and public facilities. Approximately 119,000 Oklahomans were employed by the WPA from 1935 to 1937.

ACTIVITIES

Video

The Great Depression: Crash Course US History #33

Discover more about the Great Depression by watching this video.

1. In the video, John Green observes that although the Great Depression happened after the stock market crash, this was not what caused it. How did the Great Depression start? What did Herbert Hoover do to try to fix the situation? Why did Hoover's efforts fail?
2. How did the time period that *The Grapes of Wrath* was written in impact Steinbeck's creation of the novel? In what ways might the story be different if it were written today?

Document

The American society During the Great Depression in John Steinbeck's *The Grapes of Wrath*

Review the article by Mohamed Merada about the social status of the American community during the Great Depression.

1. Who do you think is the intended audience for this document? Why? Are the tone and language used appropriate for this audience? Explain your answer.
2. What are the main points of the document and how are they presented? Are these points conveyed effectively to the reader? Why or why not?

RUBRIC

Writing a Short Story

Students will choose an excerpt from the novel and use it as their inspiration in writing a short story. An exemplary short story will meet the following criteria.

- Engages the reader from the opening line
- Establishes a clear, consistent point of view
- Introduces a narrator and a setting
- Develops an engaging conflict at the heart of the narrative to build tension and keep the reader interested
- Develops characters and events through purposeful and well-crafted literary devices
- Creates a logical progression of events in the narrative that build upon each other using various techniques
- Explores ideas, concepts, and writing styles with creativity and originality
- Demonstrates a high level of skill in using appropriate narrative techniques to tell the story
- Concludes the narrative in a thoughtful, effective manner appropriate to the narrative
- Uses varied, purposeful diction and syntax to affect style and serve the narrative
- Writes with clarity, imagination, and a unique, personal voice
- Does not use stereotypes or clichés
- Uses effective, believable dialogue
- Uses correct spelling, grammar, and punctuation

Conflict in the Novel

Conflict in literature is a struggle between two or more forces that oppose one another. When those forces collide, it creates tension that begs for resolution. This struggle is often between the protagonist and antagonist, but there are other types of conflict found in literature as well.

The Four Major Types of Conflict in Literature

MAN VS. MAN

In a man versus man conflict, the protagonist struggles against an opposing character, usually the antagonist. This is a common type of conflict in fiction, and generally features the fight between good and evil. In William Shakespeare's *Hamlet*, a young prince seeks to avenge the death of his father, who was murdered by the prince's uncle.

MAN VS. SELF

In a man versus self conflict, the protagonist fights an inner battle that is often about a major decision he or she must make. In *Star Wars Episode III: Revenge of the Sith*, a young Anakin Skywalker must decide if he will serve the powers of good or evil. He eventually becomes the villain Darth Vader.

MAN VS. SOCIETY

In a man versus society conflict, the protagonist is opposed to the principles or actions of his or her community. This conflict is based on the protagonist's beliefs or morals. In George Orwell's dystopian novel, *1984*, Winston and Julia stand against an authoritarian society run by Big Brother.

MAN VS. NATURE

In a man versus nature conflict, the protagonist faces an obstacle in nature, which may be an entire landscape or a symbolic representation of nature, such as an animal or natural disaster. In Yann Martel's *The Life of Pi*, the 16-year-old survivor of a shipwreck has to survive in a lifeboat with a large Bengal tiger.

Types of Conflict in *The Grapes of Wrath*

The two main types of conflict in *The Grapes of Wrath* are man versus society and man versus self. Both of these conflicts drive the major events of the story.

Man versus Society

"A heavy silence fell in the tent. Casy stared out the entrance, into the dark night. 'Lookie, Tom,' he said at last. 'We come to work there. They says it's gonna be fi' cents...We got there an' they says they're payin' two an' a half cents. A fella can't even eat on that, an' if he got kids—So we says we won't take it. So they druv us off. An' all the cops in the worl' come down on us. Now they're payin' you five. When they bust this here strike—ya think they'll pay five?'
'I dunno,' Tom said. 'Payin' five now.'
'Lookie,' said Casy. 'We tried to camp together, an' they druv us like pigs. Scattered us...Druv us like pigs. They run you in like pigs, too. We can't las' much longer. Some people ain't et for two days. You goin' back tonight?'
'Aim to,' said Tom.
'Well—tell the folks in there how it is, Tom. Tell 'em they're starvin' us an' stabbin' theirself in the back. 'Cause sure as cowflops she'll drop to two an' a half jus' as soon as they clear us out.'"

Chapter 26

Man versus Self

"Tom laughed uneasily, 'Well, maybe like Casy says, a fella ain't got a soul of his own, but on'y a piece of a big one—an' then—'
'Then what, Tom?'
'Then it don' matter. Then I'll be all aroun' in the dark. I'll be ever'where—wherever you look. Wherever they's a fight so hungry people can eat, I'll be there. Wherever they's a cop beatin' up a guy, I'll be there. If Casy knowed, why, I'll be in the way guys yell when they're mad an'—I'll be in the way kids laugh when they're hungry an' they know supper's ready. An' when our folks eat the stuff they raise an' live in the houses they build—why, I'll be there. See? God, I'm talkin' like Casy. Comes of thinkin' about him so much. Seems like I can see him sometimes.'"

Chapter 28

ACTIVITIES

More

The Types of Conflict in *The Grapes of Wrath*

Analyze the excerpts from the novel revealing the types of conflict as they appear in *The Grapes of Wrath*.

1. How do these excerpts of conflict reveal the novel's theme? How do they reveal character? Explain and defend your ideas.
2. Write an analysis of Steinbeck's development of Tom's inner. What deeper truths may be suggested about this character as a result of his conflict?

Document

Literary Conflict in The Grapes of Wrath

Review the cartoon by Kristy Littlehale outlining some of the conflicts in *The Grapes of Wrath*.

1. What symbols are found in the cartoon? Why are they used?
2. How would you explain the message of the cartoon? What emotions do you think the cartoonist is attempting to evoke? Give reasons for your answer.

RUBRIC

Holding a Classroom Debate

Students will form groups and prepare arguments for a debate on a controversial issue. Exemplary performance in a debate will meet the following criteria.

- Demonstrates in-depth understanding of the topic and related information
- Presents strong, logical, and convincing arguments
- Communicates in a clear and confident manner
- Maintains eye contact
- Uses clear vocal tone and a reasonable rate of vocal delivery
- Uses respectful and appropriate language and body language
- Delivers arguments, evidence, and counter-evidence in an engaging and persuasive manner
- Supports each major point of an argument with several relevant and detailed facts and examples
- Connects all arguments to the overall topic in a clear, concise, and organized manner
- Presents the arguments and supporting evidence in a clear, logical manner
- Presents clear, thorough, and accurate information throughout the debate
- Addresses all of the opposing team's arguments with counter-arguments
- Identifies any weakness in the opposing team's arguments
- Constructs strong and relevant counter-arguments using accurate information
- Presents strong and persuasive arguments throughout the debate
- Summarizes the arguments in the closing statement

Introducing the Characters

An author has several ways of developing a novel's characters. In the direct method, the reader sees the characters in action, listens to their words, and peeks into their psyche. The reader sees and hears the things the characters do, and the reasons why. When an author wants to impart important aspects of a character's personality, he or she can also do this indirectly, through other characters, thus allowing the reader to see a character through the eyes of others.

Major Characters in *The Grapes of Wrath*

Tom Joad

The main character, Tom is fresh out of prison. He learns to put his own well-being second to that of his family, and envisions a better future for the Joad household and others. He goes through the most changes of any character in the novel.

Ma Joad

Ma Joad is one of the more complicated characters in the book. She is the backbone of the Joad family, and without her, the family might not get to where they are going. Ma is a very resolute, no-nonsense type of woman who strives to keep her family together during torturous times.

Pa Joad

Pa Joad is a down-on-his-luck sharecropper whose land has just been foreclosed by the bank.

Steinbeck took great care in developing his characters, for example, in his use of Jim Casy to expound on his personal philosophical beliefs. Steinbeck created Casy as the book's moral compass. Yet, of all the characters, Tom Joad is the most developed.

Tom is the novel's chief protagonist. A decent individual, Tom tries to live life as best as he can with the cards he is dealt. Although he killed a man and spent several years in prison, Tom does not waste time thinking of the past, and he has no regrets. Tom is strong, thoughtful, and has an air of moral rectitude and certainty. He is a complex character, committed to a better future. Tom is the first character the reader meets, and as the book continues, the reader becomes deeply concerned about his life.

As critic Peter Lisca wrote in 1957, "Steinbeck's great achievement in *The Grapes of Wrath* is that while minimizing what seem to be the most essential elements of fiction—plot and character—he was able to create a well-made and emotionally compelling novel out of materials which in most other hands have resulted in sentimental **propaganda**." What makes *The Grapes of Wrath* special is that the book's most important antagonist is not a person, but the poverty which has created so much hardship. As a result, poor people have to deal with many obstacles, such as society, which includes landowners, police, and others. These groups ostracize and feel contempt for the Joads, and those like them. Nature is also an antagonist, as the drought and rough environmental conditions are killing people, or, at the very least, making it unbearably difficult for them to survive.

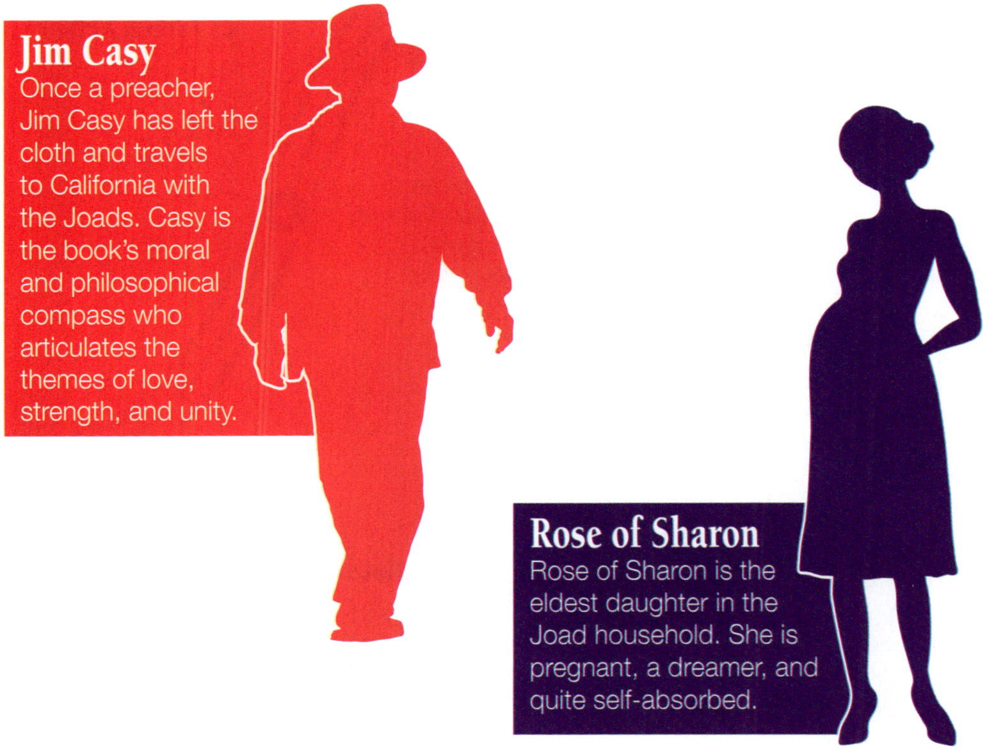

ACTIVITIES

Weblink

Character Analysis of Tom Joad

Review a character analysis of Tom Joad and debate his role in *The Grapes of Wrath*.

1. Although Tom was in prison for killing a man, this was an act of self-defense. How does this affect the reader's opinion of him? Give textual evidence to support your claims.
2. Tom begins the novel as an angry, selfish man, but by the end, he comes to value his family and becomes a man of action. Does this transformation justify his past actions? Why or why not? Support your opinion with specific examples from the text.

More

Character Development in *The Grapes of Wrath*

Analyze the characters in *The Grapes of Wrath* using the descriptions on the character map and excerpts from each character. Then, choose a character and answer the following questions.

1. Which of the writer's techniques are most effective at revealing this character's traits? Why?
2. In what ways is the characterization of this character ineffective? What could be done to improve this character's function in the novel? Defend your ideas with evidence.

RUBRIC

Creating a Literary Device Analysis Booklet

Students will analyze the author's use of a literary device in the novel, and create a booklet to present this analysis. An exemplary literary device analysis booklet will meet the following criteria.

- Defines the chosen literary device accurately and in detail
- Places the definition of the literary device at the beginning of the booklet
- Provides strong, specific examples of how this literary device is used in the novel
- Describes examples in detail, with quotations properly integrated
- Includes thorough analysis of the use, purpose, and effectiveness of each example of how the chosen literary device is used in the novel
- Arranges all pages logically
- Examples are organized chronologically
- Provides no more than one example and its analysis per page
- Creates a neat, well-organized, and attractive booklet
- Booklet is colorful and displays the student's creativity
- Uses illustrations to represent the chosen literary device and the examples of how it is used in the novel

The Art of Storytelling

Steinbeck structures *The Grapes of Wrath* in a logical way. The novel is replete with many literary devices that allow Steinbeck to tell the story, and convey the message he wants readers to understand and appreciate. For example, one of Steinbeck's techniques is to create a dark and foreboding mood throughout the novel. The mood is important because it drives home the general despair that permeates Depression-era life.

Structure of a Narrative

Every narrative has a certain structure. The most common is dramatic structure. Dramatic structure, or Freytag's Pyramid, consists of five main components, which Steinbeck uses in *The Grapes of Wrath*.

Freytag's Pyramid

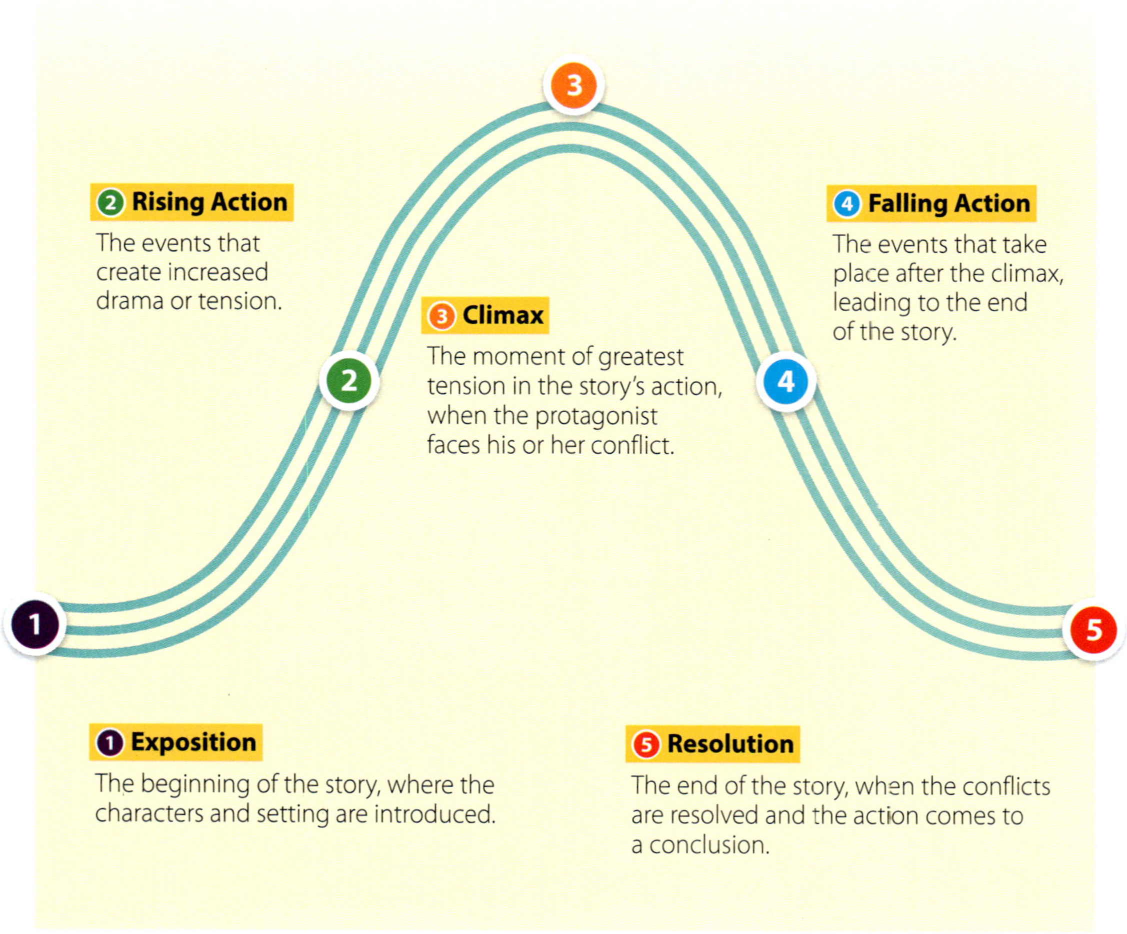

Plot

Central to every narrative is the plot, a series of actions that move the story forward. The plotline is the order in which the events, or plot points, take place. The writer uses each of these plot points, building them on one another and organizing them in a coherent fashion. Like a set of falling dominoes, each event causes the next event to happen, which bolsters the narrative.

Plot Points in Chapter 2 of *The Grapes of Wrath*

1. Tom Joad is newly released from prison.
2. It is revealed that Tom served four years at the McAlester State Penitentiary for manslaughter.
3. Tom is dressed in a cheap suit and hitches a ride with a trucker he meets at a roadside restaurant.
4. The trucker's vehicle carries a "No Riders" sign, but Tom asks the driver to be a "good guy" and give him a lift.
5. The driver starts questioning Tom.
6. Tom explains that he is returning to his father's farm.
7. The Joads have been driven off their land by a large tractor, sent by the land's owner and bankers.
8. The driver tells Tom of the things that have changed since he has been away.

Literary Devices

A literary device is any feature of literature that can be identified, studied, and analyzed. There are two types of literary devices. These are literary elements and literary techniques.

Literary Elements

Literary elements are larger features that captivate and engage a reader's imagination. All works of fiction feature various literary elements.

Mood
The mood is the overall feeling that the narrative is intended to evoke within the reader.

Moral
The moral is the lesson that is intended to be taught throughout the narrative.

Action
Action is the device through which a writer leads the reader through the story.

Literary Techniques

Literary techniques are the various ways a writer can manipulate language to convey meaning or to create a distinct style.

Personification
Personification is when an author attributes human qualities to an animal, object, or abstraction.

Metaphor
A metaphor makes a comparison by describing something in a way that is not literally true.

Allusion
An allusion is an indirect or passing reference, designed to call something to mind without actually mentioning it.

ACTIVITIES

Weblink

John Steinbeck: 19 Quotes on Writing and the Writer's Life
Examine some of Steinbeck's thoughts about writing.

1. Steinbeck claims that "[i]n every bit of honest writing in the world...there is a base theme." Why do you think he believes this to be true? How is this position evidenced in *The Grapes of Wrath*?
2. Steinbeck suggests, "if you are using dialogue—say it aloud as you write it. Only then will it have the sound of speech." How does the dialogue in The Grapes of Wrath follow this advice? In what ways might this help readers to better connect with the characters? What downfalls might this approach have and why?

More

Examples of Literary Techniques from the Novel
Analyze the author's use of literary techniques and how they contribute to the narrative of *The Grapes of Wrath*.

1. Choose one literary technique used in the novel. In what particular way did the author use this literary technique? How effective was its usage?
2. What arguments can be made for the use of your chosen literary technique in a text? If this technique were overused or underutilized, what effect might it have on an author's work?

Theme in the Novel

The theme of a story is a general, universal statement about life. Many times, themes are stated outright, but often, they are **insinuated**, allowing the reader to make certain judgments. Theme is not to be confused with the topic of a story, which is the overall subject. Themes make an observation or statement about the topic. Themes can be expressed as events, dialogue, and actions. One reader might have a different interpretation of a theme than another.

Major Themes of *The Grapes of Wrath*

Steinbeck wanted to underscore just how rotten people can be to one other. As such, inhumanity is one of the novels darkest themes. Steinbeck not only looks at the forces that separate rich into poor, but he also describes the effort the strong apply to preserve their place in the world. In one overriding sense, *The Grapes of Wrath* is a dark novel, but in another sense, it hopeful. The novel centers on the Joads, bound together by family blood, making the importance of family and friendship another theme. The Joads are a resilient people, refusing to let circumstances break their spirit and will. Steinbeck wants the reader to know that there is dignity in anger, another major theme in the novel.

Man's Inhumanity to Man

"Once California belonged to Mexico and its land to Mexicans; and a horde of tattered feverish Americans poured in. And such was their hunger for land that they took the land—stole Sutter's land, Guerrero's land, took the grants and broke them up and growled and quarreled over them, those frantic hungry men; and they guarded with guns the land they had stolen. They put up houses and barns, they turned the earth and planted crops. And these things were possession, and possession was ownership. The Mexicans were weak and fled. They could not resist, because they wanted nothing in the world as ferociously as the Americans wanted land."

Chapter 19

Importance of Family and Friendship

"Noah and Uncle John and the preacher began to unload the truck. They helped Grampa down and sat him on the ground and he sat limply, staring ahead of him. 'You sick, Grampa?' Noah asked...
Sairy Wilson walked slowly and carefully toward him. 'How'd you like ta come in our tent?' she asked. 'You kin lay down on our mattress an' rest.'
He looked up at her, drawn by her soft voice. 'Come on now,' she said. 'You'll git some rest. We'll he'p you over.'
Without warning Grampa began to cry."

Chapter 13

Dignity of Anger

"The women watched the men, watched to see whether the break had come at last. The women stood silently and watched. And where a number of men gathered together, the fear went from their faces, and anger took its place. And the women sighed with relief, for they knew it was all right—the break had not come; and the break would never come as long as fear could turn to wrath."

Chapter 29

Secondary Themes

Secondary themes add context to a novel, allowing for the narrative to become deeper and more complex. In *The Grapes of Wrath*, people are motivated by their own self-interests and greed. For example, the landowners and businessmen are motivated by their own selfishness to keep thousands of families shackled by poverty. The migrants are also guided by their own self-interests, which in their case, is survival. They band together for the collective good, sharing not only what they want out of life, but how their burdens weigh them down. **Resiliency** is also a secondary theme. The Joads are a stubborn brood, refusing to allow society to break them. In Steinbeck's world, there is dignity in such wrath. Through many trials and tribulations, including suffering many losses, the Joads maintain their self-respect in order to survive, at least spiritually.

ACTIVITIES

Weblink

Really Useful Links: All About Theme
Evaluate the article about theme by Paul FitzSimons

1. In the article, FitzSimons suggests that the best stories never directly spell out the theme. Do you agree with this assertion? Why or why not? Does Steinbeck do this in *The Grapes of Wrath*? Cite textual evidence to support your answer.
2. FitzSimons references the opinions of novelist Chuck Wendig, who believes that once a theme has been established, the other elements of the story should support this argument. How does Steinbeck use other story elements to support his themes in *The Grapes of Wrath*? Is he successful in doing so? Give specific examples from the novel.

More

Major and Secondary Themes
Analyze the author's development of themes over the course of the novel.

1. Choose a secondary theme from this spread and analyze its appearances in the novel. How does this theme first emerge? Which is the most poignant example of this theme in the novel?
2. What particular commentary might the author be making about life as a result of this theme's presence in the text? Explain and defend your ideas.
3. Choose a major theme presented on pages 16–17. In what ways does your chosen secondary theme relate to this major theme? Does it deepen or detract from the major theme? How or in what way?

RUBRIC

Creating a Symbolism Poster

Students will choose one of the other symbols listed on page 19 and analyze its role in the novel. They will then create a poster to present their analysis. An exemplary symbolism poster will meet the following criteria.

- Presents a clear purpose that is conveyed throughout the poster
- Shows an understanding of the concept of symbolism and the role it has in the novel
- Provides an in-depth analysis of what the symbol represents
- Discusses the role the symbol has in the novel
- Clearly indicates where the symbol appears in the novel
- Uses specific, detailed examples from the text to support the analysis
- Makes clear connections to the text
- Properly integrates all quotations
- Organizes the information in a logical, easy-to-read manner
- Includes high-quality graphics that relate to the symbol and effectively enhance understanding of the topic
- Features clear and concise writing
- Uses correct spelling, grammar, and punctuation
- Clearly labels items of importance
- Headings and subheadings are clear and easy to read
- Uses layout to creatively enhances the information
- Creates a poster that is attractive in terms of layout, design, and organization
- Shows a strong effort by the student

Symbolism in the Novel

Two people can read the same book and come away with two different meanings. Symbolism is a literary technique writers use to help convey the theme of a book. Writers use symbols to convey what they think or how they feel about specific events, ideas, and concepts. Symbolism also helps provide universality, or the idea that the reader can relate to a novel's events and characters. By identifying and analyzing the symbols a writer uses, the reader can gain a deeper understanding of the story.

Blood as a Symbol

There is a great deal of blood in *The Grapes of Wrath*. The title itself, taken from a Civil War-era song, invokes a bloody image as the Lord "is trampling out the vintage where the grapes of wrath are stored." The vintage is a **euphemism** for the blood spilled to "make men free," or in other words, the people that are dying to end slavery.

Blood in literature can symbolize both life and death. The bloody death of Tom's dog early in the trip westward foreshadows the tragedies that the Joad family will have to endure. The slaughter of the pigs is another poignant example of blood as a powerful symbol of oppression, death, and waste. Steinbeck asks why children die of malnutrition as food is left to rot, coffee is left to burn, and pigs are killed and tossed away.

Rose of Sharon's pregnancy, on the other hand, is poignant because it symbolizes the life-giving blood that she imparts to her unborn child. The birth represents the new life the Joads and others are seeking, while the child itself represents hope. Yet, when the baby is stillborn, the hope of such a new beginning is destroyed. However, instead of slipping into despair, the family moves on.

Where Does Blood Appear in the Novel?

Other Symbols in the Novel

The Turtle

The turtle crossing the road is one of the first symbols readers encounter. At first, the turtle appears helpless, plodding and slow as he tries to cross the road, but when a car swerves to avoid it, the turtle ducks into its shell for cover. When the truck takes aim at the animal, it hits the side of the turtle's shell, flipping it over, but the turtle is able to right itself. Steinbeck uses the turtle to portray the resilience of humanity.

Jim Casy as Jesus Christ

Jim Casy, the former preacher, is a stand-in for Jesus Christ. Jim's initials, J.C., are the same as Jesus Christ's. Like Jesus, Casy wanders in the desert and sacrifices himself for his fellow man. In Jim's case, his sacrifice is in order to save Tom after a run-in with a sheriff's deputy. Jim also becomes a martyr like Jesus. Jim even paraphrases Jesus on the cross, telling those who are about to kill him, "You don' know what you're a-doin."

Dust

The novel is set in the Dust Bowl, and as such, dust becomes a powerful symbol. It means the end of a good life and the start of bad times. Yet, kicking off the dust from one's shoes, as Tom does, ties into Steinbeck's theme of the resiliency of the human spirit.

ACTIVITIES

More

What Symbols Appear in the Novel?

Assess the author's use of symbolism in the novel.

1. Choose an example from the chart and analyze what this symbol represents. For which character is this symbol the most poignant in the novel? For which character is the symbol least poignant? Argue your opinions with clear reasons.
2. How is this symbol used or reflected in the novel's themes? Illustrate the ways in which the author's use of language deepens or weakens the meaning of the symbol. Explain and defend your ideas.

Weblink

The Complete Guide to Symbolism

Examine the blog post discussing the usage of symbolism in literature.

1. Contrast and compare examples of analytical descriptions of feelings and sensory descriptions using symbolism from the novel. Which kind is more effective in the novel? Provide reasons for your ideas.
2. Should analytical descriptions play a considerable role in the language of a novel? Why or why not?

RUBRIC

Analyzing a Video

Students will watch and assess a video related to a component of the novel, and write an analysis of the video. An exemplary video analysis will meet the following criteria.

- Identifies the purpose of the video
- Identifies the intended audience of the video
- Describes how the content of the video is presented
- Summarizes the information and opinions presented in the video
- Analyzes the quality of the content presented in the video
- Assesses the effectiveness of the video
- Discusses the technical aspects of the video and whether or not these enhance the content
- Determines whether the images and graphics used in the video relate to the content
- Determines whether the video is easy to follow and understand
- Gives the analysis a clear and consistent purpose
- Organizes the analysis in a logical, effective manner
- Presents a strong, clear argument about the video
- Provides strong and accurate details to support the argument about the video
- Considers other perspectives on the purpose and effectiveness of the video
- Makes connections between the video and the novel
- Properly integrates quotations from the video
- Cites all sources used in the analysis

The Use of Language

Steinbeck has an ear for language and uses different styles to convey several messages. *The Grapes of Wrath* is a perfect example of how Steinbeck uses realistic language to create an emotional bond with readers. Nearly all of his characters speak with a heavy **dialect**. On one level, by using such language, *The Grapes of Wrath* accurately describes the effects of impoverishment and struggle. On another level, it gives readers a sense of how people in that particular region lived and interacted with one another.

By using natural dialect, Steinbeck is able to bring his characters to life. The reader does not just read the words, but in a sense, can actually hear them, a technique which draws the reader deeper into the story. Steinbeck uses dialect the most when he is writing about the Joads. "Thinking," for example, becomes "think'in," "going to" becomes "gonna," and "family" becomes "fambly." When the Nobel Committee awarded Steinbeck the Nobel Prize in Literature in 1962, it was, "for his realistic and imaginative writings, combining as they do sympathetic humour and keen social perception."

Dialect in the Novel

"'I ain't gonna baptize. I'm gonna work in the fiel's, in the green fiel's, an' I'm gonna be near to folks. I ain't gonna try to teach 'em nothin'. I'm gonna try to learn. Gonna learn why the folks walks in the grass, gonna hear 'em talk, gonna hear 'em sing. Gonna listen to kids eatin' mush...Gonna eat with 'em an' learn.' His eyes were wet and shining. 'Gonna lay in the grass, open an' honest with anybody that'll have me. Gonna cuss an' swear an' hear the poetry of folks talkin'. All that's holy, all that's what I didn't understan'. All them things is the good things.'"

Chapter 10

Casy

Slang

In the novel, Steinbeck also uses slang, which is an informal way of speaking. Slang is used not only when the characters speak, but also in the text when no one is talking. Using slang in these instances, Steinbeck sets a dark mood and tone that conveys how angry he is at the way workers are treated, the conditions of the migrant camps, and how nature has ruined the lives of people.

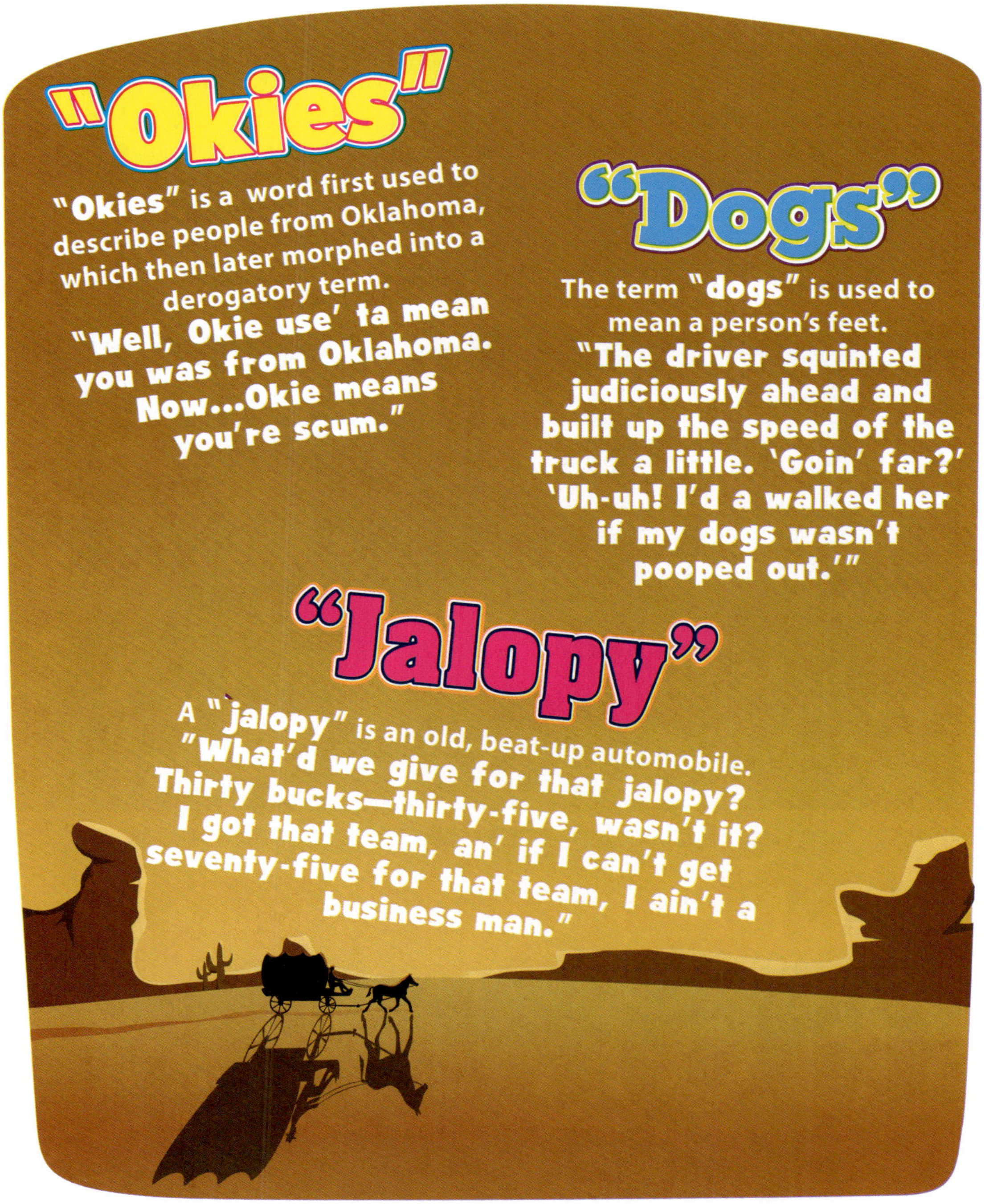

ACTIVITIES

Video

Banquet Speech by John Steinbeck (5 minutes)
Watch John Steinbeck's Nobel acceptance speech at Stockholm City Hall, from December 10, 1962.

1. In his speech, Steinbeck observes that the Nobel awards are given in part for understanding and communication, which he claims are the functions of literature. How does *The Grapes of Wrath* fulfill these functions? Give examples from the novel.
2. Steinbeck posits that literature "grew out of human need for it, and it has not changed, except to become more needed." Do you agree with this statement? Why or why not? How is Steinbeck's position evidenced in *The Grapes of Wrath*?

Weblink

The Grapes of Wrath and the language of the Dust Bowl
Explore some of the language used in the novel by reading this Oxford University Press blog post.

1. How does the language that Steinbeck uses in The Grapes of Wrath affect the reader's experience of the novel? Why do you think this is the case? Cite specific passages from the text to support your arguments.
2. It is said in the article that the great emotional influence of The Grapes of Wrath "is bound to the language of the 1930s and of the disaster which colored the decade." Do you think this is true? Why or why not? What sort of emotional influence does the novel have? Are there any other factors that contribute to this?

RUBRIC

Writing a Review

Students will write a review of the novel. An exemplary review will meet the following criteria.

- Grabs the reader's attention with a creative headline
- Begins with an engaging lead to pull the reader into the article
- Introduces the title of the novel, the author, and the genre
- Provides a brief plot description that does not give away the entire story, and makes the reader want to learn more about the novel
- Supports arguments about the novel with accurate and detailed information
- Organizes the review and its arguments in a concise, clear, and logical manner
- Fits the format and style of a review
- Follows the conventions of print or online journalism
- Demonstrates creativity in their approach
- Writes with a unique, engaging voice and perspective
- Provides fresh insight into the novel
- Provides an honest, authentic opinion on the novel
- Gives a clear recommendation on the novel, backed up by specific textual evidence
- Uses correct spelling, grammar, and punctuation

Impact of the Novel at the Time of Publishing

The Grapes of Wrath had an enormous impact when it was first published in 1939. It was the best-selling book of the year, and 430,000 copies had been printed by February 1940. Some have called it the "Great American Novel." The book's popularity was due in part to the fact that many Americans at that time were living the life of the Joads, and were **disillusioned**, angry, and bitter, yet hopeful that their lot in life would one day become better. "There are a few novelists writing as well as Steinbeck and perhaps a very few who write better," claimed Peter Monro Jack in *The New York Times* on April 16, 1939. Jack argued that "...for the present instance, Steinbeck's '*Grapes of Wrath*,' [is] as pitiful and angry a novel ever to be written about America."

Burned and Banned

The Associated Farmers of California did not like *The Grapes of Wrath* when it hit bookstore shelves. The organization called it a "pack of lies" and "communist propaganda." Many libraries banned the book and some communities even burned it in their town squares.

The Mother Road

As the Joads travel to California, they take Route 66, a two-lane, 2,448-mile (3,940-km) road stretching from Chicago to Los Angeles. Steinbeck called the highway the "Mother Road" because Route 66 was an important symbol for migrants trekking west. The book's popularity made the road a symbol of rebirth, and many people still refer to Route 66 as the Mother Road.

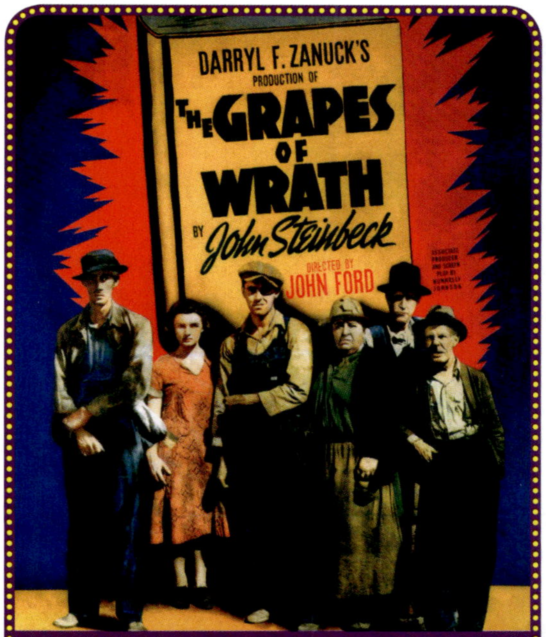

Hollywood's Version

The Grapes of Wrath was adapted for film in 1940 and directed by John Ford. Frank S. Nugent, a critic for *The New York Times*, said of the film, "In the vast library where the celluloid literature of the screen is stored, there is one small, uncrowded shelf devoted to the cinema's masterworks, to those films which by dignity of theme and excellence of treatment seem to be of enduring artistry...To that shelf of screen classics Twentieth Century-Fox yesterday added its version of John Steinbeck's *The Grapes of Wrath*."

Climate and Human Influence

The Grapes of Wrath discusses the relationship between people and the land, which was a growing concern during the Great Depression. During the 1920s and the early 1930s, there was little regard for the environmental degradation humans were inflicting. Farmers, concerned with increasing crop yields, were uprooting grasses and over-cultivating the land, which exposed the topsoil. As a result, when a drought descended over the Great Plains, the wind created huge clouds of dust, ripping topsoil from the land and tossing it into the sky. Farms withered and livelihoods sank.

ACTIVITIES

Document

John Steinbeck's New Novel Brims With Anger and Pity

Analyze the review from *The New York Times* by Peter Monro Jack, published on April 16, 1939.

1. Jack argues that despite the novel's length, "it reads as if it had been composed in a flash, ripped off the typewriter and delivered to the public as an ultimatum." How does Steinbeck manage to accomplish this? What is the ultimatum he is giving? Give reasons for your answer.
2. According to Jack, "Steinbeck has written a novel from the depths of his heart with a sincerity seldom equaled." Why do you think this is this significant? Do you agree with this assertion? Defend your opinion with solid arguments.

Weblink

'Grapes Of Wrath' And The Politics of Book Burning

Find out more about the novel's initial critical reception in this National Public Radio post.

1. The article cites Judith Krug of the American Library Association, who claims that the people who advocate for the banning and burning of books are "not afraid of the book; they're afraid of the ideas." Why do you think this is the case? What ideas in *The Grapes of Wrath* might have inspired such fear?
2. Librarian Gretchen Knief, who stood up to county supervisors in an attempt to overturn the ban, is quoted as saying that "banning books is so utterly hopeless and futile. Ideas don't die because a book is forbidden reading." Would you agree with this assessment? Why or why not?

Impact of the Novel Now

Nearly eight decades after it was first published, *The Grapes of Wrath* is still an important novel, and the book's central themes against big business and people's inhumanity still resonate. For instance, large banks continue to evict people from their homes today, even as these institutions have accepted government bailouts to keep running. In the minds of many, banks plague people with insurmountable debt that keeps them in economic chains. Susan Shillinglaw, a professor of English at San Jose State University and a Steinbeck scholar, views *The Grapes of Wrath* as timeless, claiming that the issues that resonated during the Great Depression, including economic disparity, are still front and center today.

Travels Along the Mother Road

In 2013, the National Steinbeck Center in California sent three artists to retrace the path of the Joads to commemorate the 75th anniversary of the novel. Among the artists was filmmaker P.J. Palmer, who filmed a documentary about the journey. His film revealed the struggles of dispossessed families who still live along the route.

The Grapes of Wrath has sold **more than 15 million** copies since it was **first published**.

The **first edition** of the hardcover book, published by **Viking Press**, was **619 pages** long.

The book originally cost **$2.75**, but today, a first edition is worth upwards of **$15,000**, depending on its condition.

The Ghost of Tom Joad

In 1995, musician Bruce Springsteen resurrected Tom Joad for a whole new generation in the song, *The Ghost of Tom Joad*, which he wrote after witnessing migrant workers dealing with the same social and economic issues Tom Joad went through in *The Grapes of Wrath*. "If you go to my hometown, in Freehold, there's tremendous Hispanic influence, and that was California fifteen years ago," Springsteen told *Rolling Stone* magazine in a 2007 interview. "So, when I wrote *The Ghost of Tom Joad* and wrote a lot about what was going on, it felt like 'This is what the country's going to look like in another ten or fifteen years.'"

Grapes and Opera

The Grapes of Wrath, an Opera in Three Acts was written by Ricky Ian Gordon and Michael Korie. It premiered at the Minnesota Opera in St. Paul in 2007. Songs such as *The Last Time There was Rain* and *Hooverville* punctuated the opera, giving theatergoers a sense of what life was like in the Dust Bowl. A review in *The New York Times* said that Gordon illustrated the plight of the Joads and those around them with "grace and flair" and that "Mr. Korie's literate, often clever libretto is a big help. Together, the two men gently push the narrative from episode to episode."

Clash of Classes and Culture

Many people migrated to California during the Great Depression, and those already living there saw migrant families every day. Dorothy Wallace, who lived in Salinas at the time, remembers what her neighbors were thinking. In an interview with *National Geographic* in 2014, which marked the 75th anniversary of the novel, she said, "If you were making money, you didn't like [Steinbeck]. If you were coming up through the classes, you were a fan of him. But even those that disliked him respected his writing. He just wrote things as they really were. I remember everything as the way he wrote it."

NATIONAL GEOGRAPHIC™

ACTIVITIES

Video

CSUB Celebrates the 75th Anniversary of the Grapes of Wrath

Learn more about the real-life victims of the Dust Bowl by watching this video.

1. Why are there still hard feelings about the way people were treated during the Dust Bowl? How do the first hand accounts of the people in the video affect your perception of what things were really like at that time? What does this add to your understanding of the novel?
2. Why is it so important to remember the events of the past? How is the plight of the farmer still pertinent in today's world? In what ways can The Grapes of Wrath be used to make the country a better place?

Document

DAYS OF "WRATH"

Analyze the review by Cliff Froehlich, exploring his views on *The Grapes of Wrath*.

1. What is the tone of the review? Froehlich says that the novel "continues to transport us to relevant and revelatory destinations," 75 years after its original publication. How do you think the novel is relevant to modern readers? What revelations does it inspire?
2. In what ways is the story of the Joad family universal? How might particular groups of people, such as "Americans forced from their homes by the foreclosures of the subprime mortgage crisis and the Mexicans crossing the Sonoran Desert in desperate search of work and better prospects" relate to the Joads?

RUBRIC

Creating a Timeline

Students will explore a topic related to the novel and create a timeline to present their research on historical events connected to this topic. An exemplary timeline will meet the following criteria.

- Includes the most significant events pertaining to the topic to be compared and analyzed
- Includes interesting events
- Uses accurate information for all events, including date, location, and major details
- Orders the events in a chronological sequence
- Describes each event with accurate, vivid, and specific details
- Presents the topic from three or more perspectives
- Inspires the reader to ask thoughtful questions regarding the events and perspectives presented in the timeline
- Uses correct spelling, grammar, and punctuation
- Presents the timeline in a visually attractive and striking manner
- Presents the timeline in a neat, organized manner that is logical and easy to follow
- Uses creativity to present the timeline in an engaging manner
- Effectively communicates the historical information relating to the topic
- Supports each event with reliable sources
- Expresses a clear purpose for creating the timeline
- Enhances the reader's understanding of the topic
- Includes a correctly formatted bibliography of all sources used to create the timeline

Perspectives on Economic Uncertainty in the United States

Since its founding in 1776, the United States has been through about 50 economic **recessions**. Such economic downturns are often marked by a drop in the stock market, an increase in unemployment, soaring prices, and a sluggish housing market. Over the years, many factors have contributed to economic uncertainty in the United States. **Inflation** is one of those factors.

Timeline of Major Recessions in the United States

1940s | 1950s | 1960s | 1970s

1945 A recession begins in February and lasts until October, mainly occurring because the country is transitioning to a peacetime economy following World War II.

1948–1949 An 11-month economic downturn begins in November 1948 and lasts until October 1949, when unemployment peaks at 7.9 percent.

1953–1954 Beginning in July 1953 and lasting until May 1954, this recession takes place in part due to a decrease in defense spending after the end of the Korean War. Unemployment peaks at 6.1 percent.

1957–1958 The nation's unemployment rate peaks at 7.5 percent during a recession that begins in August 1957 and lasts until April 1958.

1960 Beginning in April and lasting 10 months, this recession ends when President John F. Kennedy uses the government to stimulate spending, which creates jobs for many people.

As inflation increases, prices for food, automobiles, and other commodities increase. As a result, the percentage of goods and services that a person can purchase with the same amount of money becomes lower and lower. Falling wages are another contributor to economic uncertainty.

High interest rates can also cause a recession. When interest rates on loans are high, the amount of money people and companies can invest is limited. As a result, factories do not upgrade their equipment or hire workers because there is not a great demand for their products. Moreover, the general public finds it increasingly expensive to borrow money to buy homes, cars, and other major items.

1973–1975 When the Organization of the Petroleum Exporting Countries (OPEC) stops exporting oil to the United States, the U.S. economy goes into a 16-month tailspin.

2007–2009 Known as the Great Recession, this 18-month downturn is the worst economic crisis since the Great Depression. During the Great Recession, home prices fall, and millions lose their homes and jobs.

1980s | 1990s | 2000s

1980–1982 This recession is actually two economic downturns. The first lasts from January to July 1980, and the second lasts 16 months, from July 1981 to November 1982.

2001 An eight-month recession begins in March and lasts until November. This turndown is caused by the boom and then bust of technology and Internet stocks, and is worsened by terrorist attacks on September 11, 2001.

ACTIVITIES

Transparency–Timeline

Timeline of Major Recessions in the United States

Examine the historical and cultural contexts shown on the timeline. Then, contrast and correlate its elements with the themes and events presented in *The Grapes of Wrath*.

1. In what ways can historical events, culture, and social mores influence a population's perspective on economic uncertainty? How might these elements have shaped the way a reader in the 1940s interpreted the novel?
2. How might the era in which John Steinbeck wrote *The Grapes of Wrath* have influenced the novel's themes and settings? Where in the novel is this most evident? Explain your reasoning.
3. Which current events, changes in laws, new ideas, or political discussions are shaping the economy in the United States today? Which ideas and attitudes are still prevailing? Why?
4. How might current events and present perspectives affect the way a reader interprets the novel? Why is it important for readers to understand the era and context in which a novel is written?

RUBRIC

Writing a Comparative Essay

Students will compare two literary devices used in the novel, and then write a comparative essay based on their analysis. An exemplary comparative essay will meet the following criteria.

- Consists of a one-paragraph introduction, three body paragraphs, and a one-paragraph conclusion
- Introduction includes an engaging lead statement about the topic of the essay, more detailed information about the novel, and a one-sentence thesis that specifically states the essay's argument
- Body paragraphs include a topic sentence that refers to the thesis and how the idea appears in the novel, a supporting sentence that points to this part of the novel, textual evidence of this idea from the novel, and analysis of this evidence
- Body paragraphs end with a transition to the next paragraph
- Conclusion refers to the topic of the essay and the three points presented in the body paragraphs, and restates the thesis
- Provides a thorough analysis of the literary devices in question
- Cites strong and thorough textual evidence to support analysis of what the novel says explicitly
- Presents a clear, specific thesis that indicates a high level of critical engagement
- Organizes ideas in a logical manner
- Communicates arguments in a clear, effective manner
- Properly integrates all quotations
- Correctly cites all sources used
- Correctly formats bibliography

Writing a Comparative Essay

The Grapes of Wrath features a number of characters and themes that are still important today. Once you are done reading, write a comparative essay to explore how Steinbeck uses two literary devices to move the novel forward. This could be a comparison of characters, themes, symbols, or settings. To write a comparative essay, you will need to formulate an argument, which should clearly state how you feel your compared elements are similar or different. Support your argument with sufficient evidence from the novel and valid reasoning.

How to Analyze and Compare Characters

Use the chart below to guide your comparison of two characters in *The Grapes of Wrath*.

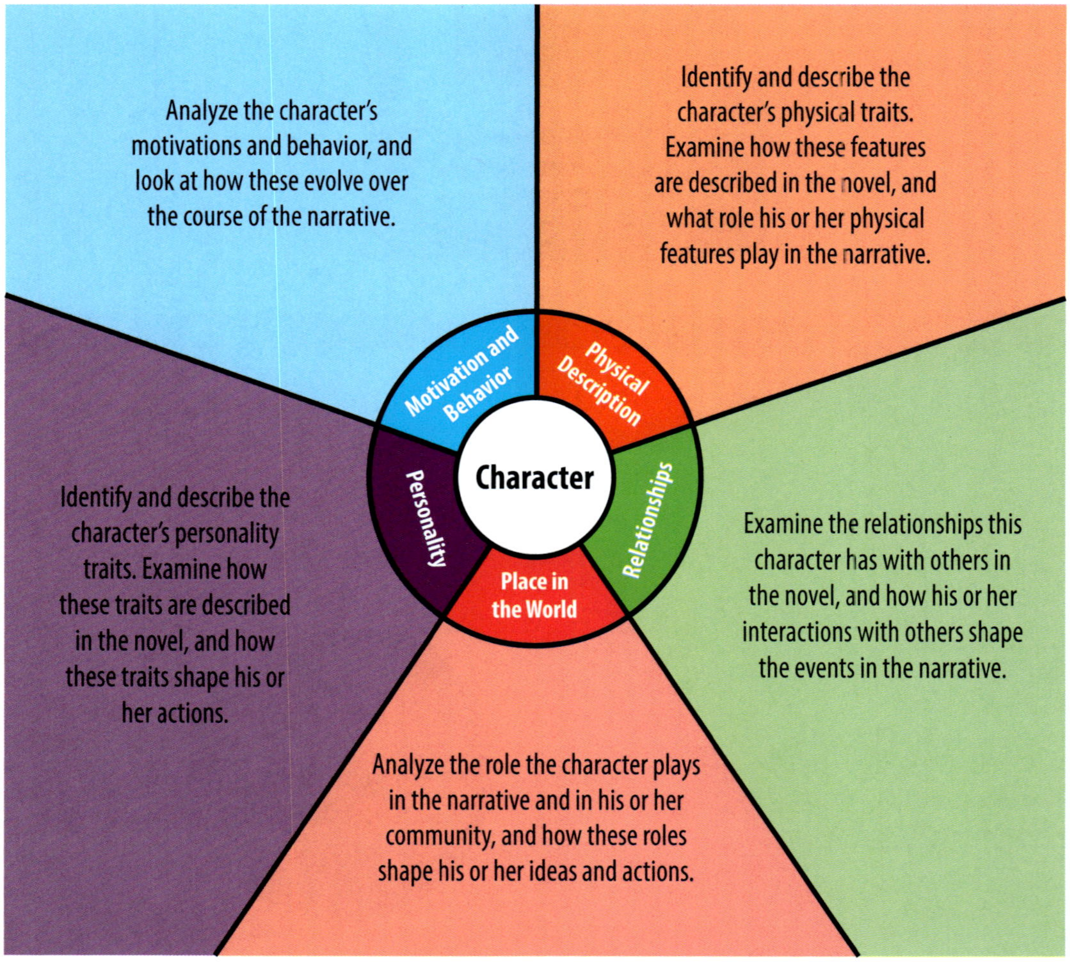

Comparing Tom Joad and Ma Joad

Tom Joad

Relationships
- Son
- Brother
- Friend
- Grandson
- Disciple to Jim Casy

Motivation and Behavior
- Uses his energies in the present moment
- The future does not concern him
- Slowly abandons his private thoughts
- Does not want to be a silent witness to injustice
- Sets out to help people

Place in the World
- Protagonist of the novel
- Son of Ma and Pa Joad
- Friend
- Fighter for justice

Personality
- Kind
- Merciful
- Quick to anger
- Pragmatic
- Philosophical
- Thoughtful
- Compassionate

Physical Description
- Not more than age 30
- Hint of brown in his eyes
- Upper lip is long
- Protruding teeth
- Broad fingers

Ma Joad

Place in the World
- Cornerstone and unofficial head of the family

Motivation and Behavior
- Wants to hold her family together
- Wants to provide comfort
- Wants to help each family member
- Works to gain people's trust

Relationships
- Mother of Tom, Rose of Sharron, and Noah
- Wife of Pa Joad

Personality
- Hopeful
- Calm
- Intuitive
- Nurturing
- Leader
- Protective
- Emotional healer

Physical Description
- Older
- Steel-gray hair
- Freckled arms
- Delicate hands
- Full, kind face

More

Questions for Character Analysis

Analyze how specific character features, such as conflicts, motivations, relationships, place in the world, and personality affect the plot of *The Grapes of Wrath*. Cite strong and thorough textual evidence to support your analysis of what the novel says explicitly as well as the inferences you may have drawn from the novel's setting, themes, and symbols.

Quiz Answers

1. A
2. B
3. B
4. B
5. D
6. B
7. D
8. C
9. A
10. A

Key Words

dabbled: experimented with

dialect: how people in different regions speak

disillusioned: disappointed in someone or something that is not as good or true as a person had believed

dispossessed: when people are deprived of something they own, such as land or property

euphemism: an indirect word or phrase substituted in place of one considered too blunt in reference to something unpleasant

inflation: price increases of goods and services over time

insinuated: suggested or hinted that something is bad or unpleasant

pommeled: pummeled or hit

propaganda: biased information that is used to publicize and promote a particular political cause or point of view

recessions: temporary downswings in the economy that may last for months or years

resiliency: when someone can recover from difficult conditions or circumstances in life

verdant: green; lush with vegetation

Literary Terms

action: everything that occurs in a narrative

antagonist: the character who stands in opposition to the protagonist; in some cases, the antagonist creates or represents the conflict that the protagonist faces

characterization: the act of describing a character through the person's appearance and personality

climax: the moment of greatest tension in the story's action

conflict: a struggle between two or more opposing forces, creating a tension that must be resolved

exposition: the beginning of the story, where the characters and setting are introduced

falling action: the events that take place after the climax, leading up to the resolution of the story

Freytag's Pyramid: a narrative structure consisting of five elements; this includes exposition, rising action, climax, falling action, and resolution

narrative: a logically arranged series of events presented for an audience; a story

plot: the events that take place in a story

protagonist: the person or thing that acts in opposition to the antagonist

resolution: the end of the story, when the problems are resolved and the action comes to a conclusion

rising action: the events that create increased drama or tension

simile: a comparison between two things using the word "like" or "as"

symbolism: a stylistic device using symbols to represent and intensify concepts and ideas

Index

1984 10

allusion 15
anger 29
antagonist 10, 13

blood 18, 19

California 4, 5, 6, 9, 13, 16, 22, 24, 25
Cannery Row 5
characters 10, 12, 13, 14, 15, 18, 20, 21, 28
Christ, Jesus 19
Civilian Conservation Corp (CCC) 9
climate 23
communist 22
conflict 10, 11, 14
Cup of Gold 5

dialogue 16
dust 6, 7, 19, 23
Dust Bowl 6, 7, 19, 25
dystopian 10

East of Eden 5

Fonda, Henry 5
Freytag's pyramid 14

Great Depression 5, 6, 8, 9, 23, 24, 25, 27

Hamlet 10
Henning, Carol 5
Hoover, Herbert 9
Hoovervilles 9, 25

Life of Pi, The 10
Lisca, Peter 13

Martel, Yann 10
metaphor 15
migration 6, 25
mood 5, 14, 15, 21
moral 10, 13, 15
Mother Road 22, 24

narrative 14, 15, 17, 25, 28
National Steinbeck Center 24
New Deal 9
New York 4, 5
New York Times, The 22, 23, 25
Nobel Prize 20

Okies 21
Oklahoma 4, 5, 6, 9, 21
Orwell, George 10

Palmer, P.J. 24
personification 15
plot 13, 15
propaganda 13, 22
protagonist 10, 12, 13, 14, 29
Pulitzer Prize 5

recessions 26, 27
Roosevelt, Franklin D. 9
Route 66 6, 22, 24

Shakespeare, William 10
Shillinglaw, Susan 24
slang 21
Springsteen, Bruce 25
Star Wars Episode III: Revenge of the Sith 10
Steinbeck, John 4, 5, 6, 13, 14, 16, 17, 18, 19, 20, 21, 22, 23, 24, 25, 28
Steinbeck, John Ernst 4
Steinbeck, Olive 4
symbolism 10, 18, 19, 22, 28

themes 13, 15, 16, 17, 18, 19, 23, 24, 28
Tortilla Flat 5

Winter of our Discontent, The 5
Works Progress Administration (WPA) 9

LIGHTBOX

SUPPLEMENTARY RESOURCES

Click on the plus icon found in the bottom left corner of each spread to open additional teacher resources.

- Download and print the book's quizzes and activities
- Access curriculum correlations
- Explore additional web applications that enhance the Lightbox experience

LIGHTBOX DIGITAL TITLES

Packed full of integrated media

VIDEOS

INTERACTIVE MAPS

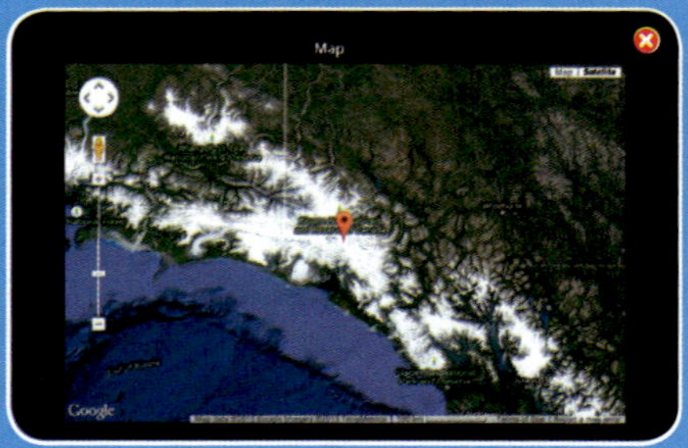

WEBLINKS

SLIDESHOWS

QUIZZES

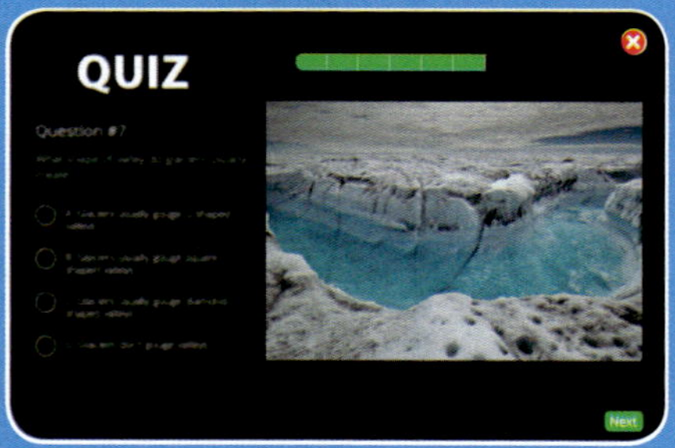

OPTIMIZED FOR

- ✓ TABLETS
- ✓ WHITEBOARDS
- ✓ COMPUTERS
- ✓ AND MUCH MORE!

Published by Smartbook Media Inc.
350 5th Avenue, 59th Floor New York, NY 10118
Website: www.openlightbox.com

Library of Congress Control Number: 2018932276

ISBN 978-1-5105-3698-2 (hardcover)
ISBN 978-1-5105-3699-9 (multi-user eBook)

Printed in Brainerd, Minnesota, United States
1 2 3 4 5 6 7 8 9 0 22 21 20 19 18

062018
121017

Editor: Katie Gillespie
Art Director: Terry Paulhus

Every reasonable effort has been made to trace ownership and to obtain permission to reprint copyright material. The publisher would pleased to have any errors or omissions brought to its attention so th they may be corrected in subsequent printings.

The publisher acknowledges Getty Images, iStock, Alamy, and Wikimedia Commons as its primary image suppliers for this title.